The *GUSTO POWER*® Workbook

Tactics and Strategies

for the Multi-Passionate Professional™

GILAT BEN-DOR

A *GUSTO POWER*™ Book

Published by Gilat Ben-Dor Media, LLC
6501 E. Greenway Pkwy., Suite 103
PMB 519
Scottsdale, AZ 85254
USA
http://GilatMedia.com

Copyright ©2011 Gilat Ben-Dor
All rights reserved.

No part of this book may be reproduced, stored in a retrieval system, or transmitted in any language, by any means, electronic, photocopying, recording, or otherwise, without written permission from the publisher.

The Gusto Power Workbook, *Multi-Passionate Professional*, and *Gilat Ben-Dor Media* are trademarks of Gilat Ben-Dor and Gilat Ben-Dor Media, LLC. *Gusto Power* is a registered trademark of Gilat Ben-Dor.

Cover design and interior layout by Gilat Ben-Dor.

For information and discounts on bulk purchases, please contact
Gilat Ben-Dor Media, LLC at address above, or email: info@GilatMedia.com

ISBN-13: 978-0-9832674-1-6
ISBN-10: 0-983267-41-3

First printed in 2011.

10 9 8 7 6 5 4 3 2 1

Printed in the U.S.A.

Committing your goals to paper increases the likelihood of your achieving them by one thousand percent.

-Brian Tracy

Additional Titles by Gilat Ben-Dor

The Confetti Path: 101 Ways to Celebrate Your Passions and Inspire Creativity

The Rainbow Blueprint: An Action Journal for Those with Many Passions

♦♦♦♦♦

For a complete list of Gilat Ben-Dor's publications since the last printing of this book, please visit http://GilatMedia.com

The *GUSTO POWER*® Workbook

Tactics and Strategies

for the Multi-Passionate Professional™

GILAT BEN-DOR

The *GUSTO POWER*® Workbook
Table of Contents

Introduction 1

How to Use This Workbook 5

Plugging the Energy Leaks 7

Ideas into Action: Reflective Planning 13

Your Personal Passion Blend 15

The Master Venture List 21

The Passion Priority Matrix & Weekly Assessments 27

Wrap-Up Review 137

About the Author 141

Additional Opportunities 143

Introduction

Chances are that if you are reading this, you are an individual with numerous interests, talents, and passions, and the desire to explore them all. In theory, this is a beautiful thing! Having a natural curiosity for many things, and the capacity (and talent) to fulfill each idea is truly a gift—to yourself, your organization, and your community, both personally and professionally. The trick is knowing how to navigate productively between these various desires. How do you actually accomplish something of value in each of these areas, instead of forever dabbling in an earnest attempt to manage it all—but ultimately, spinning your wheels and getting nowhere?

Your passions may compete with each other for your time, attention, and priorities—perhaps even blurring the lines between your personal and professional life (again, not necessarily a bad thing). You know you could achieve explosive success in your life and your career, if only you could gain clarity and direction—and yet, you want to be true to yourself, and the many passions and talents that make up who you are.

One approach that has often been used to "tame" the "scattered" multi-passionate person and their "unruly" list of diverse talents—a method that does not always work well—is what I call the Pick and Stick Approach, as in, "Just pick one thing and stick with it!" You may have heard this one aimed at you before (and have bristled at it). This approach may seem like a practical, no-brainer solution for those dispensing this advice, but as with all things, consider the source.

Most likely, this advice was given by someone who is not a Multi-Passionate Professional™ themselves and cannot imagine why one would want to obstruct the "straight and narrow" path to their idea of success (usually in a single field); or else they are masking their own spectrum of interests under the societal belief that focusing ruthlessly on The One Thing is the ticket to credibility, stability, and success.

Sure, if someone only wanted to pursue one avenue from the time they were little, then the Pick and Stick Approach would work well—both from a practical standpoint, and in keeping with their own, true desires. But telling the genuine Multi-Passionate Professional that they must choose Just One Thing from among several options is like forcing them to choose from among their children. Each may be vastly different, but you cannot imagine life without any of them now that they are a part of world.

So could someone navigate 20 different passions at once? Certainly there are limits of time, resources, and energy—but the point is that there should be no shame about being a person that may, in fact, *have* 20 different passions! Through this workbook, we will address the issue of incorporating multiple passions into your daily lifestyle, and finding the rhythm that will work best practically, while still honoring your core passions.

But back to the Pick and Stick Approach, and why it doesn't work in our case. It usually helps if Multi-Passionate Professionals (let's call them MPPs for short) are coached by a fellow MPP (who is a qualified coach and has evolved past any MPP "stuck" phases), or by other qualified professionals who understand just how important each passion is to that individual. Saying to someone who loves singing and landscape photography and leadership research and Italian language and culture that they have "too many" passions, that they must only pick one passion to focus on and "just forget the rest," is a recipe for resentment, frustration, insult, or dejection on the part of the MPP that takes this advice to heart.

Coaching MPPs vastly differs from conventional "life coaching" or traditional solution-based consulting. As an individual with numerous passions, you do not need someone prodding you along to find something you are passionate about: you have multiple callings already. Nor do you need help getting motivated: you are probably a high-energy, driven individual who is frustrated by this apparent delay in moving forward. You never asked to be in this predicament of feeling torn, or stuck in a state of analysis paralysis. You know what you want, which involves many moving parts. You also know that with a bit of clarity and a practical plan, you would propel ahead so quickly, so powerfully, that the world could not stop you.

And so, you have come to the right place. The GUSTO POWER® Workbook: Tactics and Strategies for the Multi-Passionate Professional™, is an extension of the GUSTO POWER® leadership development and coaching program I have created, specifically for gifted and motivated Multi-Passionate Professionals just like you. This workbook offers you practical advice, hands-on exercises, and a birds-eye overview of living—and succeeding—with a plate brimming with diverse endeavors.

As a Multi-Passionate Professional, you are not alone; just widely misunderstood, in a society that promotes single-focus specialization and linear progressions. With this workbook as a primary tool, you will begin to create a clear vision and an action plan for yourself, figuring out which areas would be best to expand upon and which to narrow—while also delving inward to uncover saboteurs. In this process, you will discover the essential energy leaks that have been holding you back even more than any scheduling dilemma.

If you are earnest in completing the exercises in this workbook, are open for change, and are honest with yourself as you answer tough questions, you are on your way to igniting a marked transformation in how you view yourself and your passions, how you live your life, and how you view your career. In this new frame of mind, you will be able to reclaim your sense of control, direction, and "go-getterness" that you know is inside. And you may just find yourself smiling and nodding in relief, as you whisper that triumphant word…"Finally!"

And then there will be no stopping you…

To your multi-passionate success,

Gilat Ben-Dor

How to Use This Workbook

The GUSTO POWER® Workbook: Tactics and Strategies for the Multi-Passionate Professional™ is designed to be a hands-on tool as much as a planning device. Go ahead and freely write, highlight, fold, sticky-note, scribble, and color code the charts and blanks in this workbook, and make them personal to you. Rather than feel that this workbook has been "used up" once the blanks have been filled, hold on to it and use it as a valuable reference: a view into where you came from and where you are going; a reflection of all that you have learned, and all that you are quickly becoming.

While you are welcome to skip around this workbook, I designed the sections to build upon each other and work sequentially, so going "by the book" has its merits, too. You will find a series of exercises that represent a guided process of narrowing and expansion, with additional points to consider along the way.

We first begin with *Plugging the Energy Leaks*, an in-depth look into current beliefs or situations that may be holding you back in surprising ways. These "leaks" may be small or large, relating to the past or the present; they may be obvious or subtle, involving yourself or others. Identifying—and then eradicating—these leaks is the first step towards re-setting your agenda and re-building your life with passion(s) and direction.

Next, you will experience *Ideas into Action: Reflective Planning*. Just as important as the "doing" is the "planning." Here, planning means anything but simply dreaming about, imagining, and talking about what you would really love to do if only….This is your time to lay out a blueprint that will match your ultimate objectives. If you would like to explore the idea of blueprinting further, I recommend you cross-reference this workbook with *The Rainbow Blueprint: An Action Journal for Those with Many Passions,* also from the GUSTO POWER® series. (see RainbowBlueprint.com).

Ideas into Action is followed by a multi-stepped (and fun) process, the process of forming *Your Personal Passion Blend.* You will discover the key components you value, and will have the opportunity to find meaningful ways of combining these for professional growth and personal expression.

As a multi-passionate professional, you are used to numerous ideas and new inspirations buzzing around in your head at any given day. You value these creative gems, but where do you store them? In your mind alone? This can take up valuable mental "real estate." In the *Master Venture List* exercise, you participate in an unloading and organizing of these thoughts and plans, while still keeping them safe and accessible. Your *Master Venture List* is reminiscent of a Bucket List (a lifetime goal list), but incorporates a variety of methods, and is designed especially for you.

Finally, you will reach the heart of this workbook, the culmination of all of your careful preparations: experience *The Passion Priority Matrix and Weekly Summaries*. Here is your chance to take the discoveries, preferences and developments you have worked on and implement them into a practical and enduring method.

This is a plan that you implement and revise each and every week. Comprised of 52 weekly plans, you will chart out your passions based on calibrated priorities, both *among* your various Core Passions and *within* each passion (as Passion Sub-Tasks). The beauty of these weekly plans is that you control the intensity and depth of focus of each passion. You direct this organized system which can then be revised or continued from one week to the next.

And remember to complete the *Wrap-Up Review* at the end of the workbook. You may be astonished to find how much you have grown, accomplished, and implemented when it comes to living life as a talented Multi-Passionate Professional.

Let's get started!

Plugging the Energy Leaks

If you seriously want to accomplish many things—not just dabble here and there, but truly make headway in the areas of your passions—then you will need the energy to do what it takes. In order to pursue your passions with productivity and depth, you need to have enough energy, pep, and clarity of mind to track, plan, balance, execute, and continually revise all the moving parts that are involved in such a lifestyle. Can it be done? Absolutely. I would not be writing books about pursuing multiple passions if I did not live this lifestyle successfully myself.

I know of a consultant that is hired by companies all over the world to help them save millions of dollars. One of the first things he does is look for leaks in their spending, where money is squandered redundantly or inefficiently. By finding these "leaks" and plugging them in with new solutions, the company emerges richer—and they didn't have to do anything except figure out how to stop existing leaks!

For the creative, multi-passionate professional, energy is our currency. Therefore, the first thing to do is to figure out our energy leaks. Remember: energy leaks are not necessarily the same as time leaks (i.e., pockets of wasted time), although there can be cases of overlap in these areas. Not all areas that take up time are bad: For instance, if you hold a full-time job that keeps you from pursuing all of your passions at once, but you need the job in order to pay bills (and fund some of your passions), then this is probably an endeavor worth holding onto for the moment. And, depending on the job, it may or may not be an energy leak.

Unlike the strong emotional drain of an energy leak, a time leak can be solved more easily. If you find that you do your best work between 10 am and noon, you can decline a friend's invitation for coffee, or a non-essential networking event, if it falls in that time block. Meetings, carpooling, and even meal times can often be altered to suit your needs with no more than the act of speaking up and requesting the changes. You do not have to explain yourself; simply decline due to a scheduling conflict, which is exactly the case.

On the other hand, energy leaks are far more insidious and harmful to your passion-proliferation mission. **Energy leaks can:**

- Appear spontaneously or without immediate notice

- Be tied to an uncomfortable social obligation or workplace politics

- Include triggers that happen quickly but leave lingering effects

- Elicit strong emotional reactions from you and others

- Affect your productivity, mood, focus, and creativity

It is critical to first identify, and then rid yourself of, these energy leaks to preserve your precious energy for your most important pursuits.

So where are these energy leaks lurking? Examples of energy leaks may include one or more of the following (plus others not listed):

- Petty but frequent arguments with family members, partners, co-workers, etc.

- Caving into demands on your time, where you do not or cannot decline

- Unresolved anger towards a partner, ex-partner, boss, family member, etc.

- Friends, family, colleagues, or a partner that emotionally drains you

- A cluttered environment (may be compounded if shared with someone who is the "messier" person)

- Excessive noise or darkness/brightness in your home or workplace

- Spending required time with a person or people you dislike

- Dealing frequently with broken or faulty items (i.e., a car that keeps breaking down)

- Lack of adequate sleep

- Lagging health

These are just some general examples that could cause energy leaks. The common thread is not the specifics of each situation, but the end result. All of these situations could result in feelings of anger, resentment, irritability, loss of control, futility…you get the idea. None of these feelings help the cause of clearing out your mental, emotional, and physical space in order to construct a life of integrated activities surrounding your passions.

Now it is your turn. Think about the energy leaks in your life at the moment—the smallest thing and the biggest—and write them down. If you start to feel angry or annoyed at the very thought of these situations, don't worry: this is normal. While this is not one of the most joyous exercises, it is necessary for your growth (like broccoli) and for clearing out the old to make room for new experiences (like cleaning out a closet after 12 years).

My energy leaks include:

_____
_____
_____
_____
_____
_____
_____
_____

All of those items you listed are pretty annoying, aren't they? So what should we do about them?

Here are a few suggestions for ridding yourself of energy leaks starting today. Customize these solutions to fit your own needs and situations.

1. **Reduce the sources of drama in your life.**

I will start by _____
_____
_____
_____

2. **Envision your end result: how would your life look ideally?**

What would the perfect day, week, or month be like if you were living out your life with your favorite passions?

For me, an ideal day of multi-passionate living would involve:

_____
_____

For me, an ideal week of multi-passionate living would involve:

For me, an ideal month of multi-passionate living would involve:

3. **Think ahead and imagine an exciting future based on the changes you make now.**

In one year from now, I would like to look back and see that I've accomplished these things:

4. **Resolve current relationship conflicts that are holding you back.**

Who do you need to forgive, or to whom do you owe an apology? Which situation or injustices can you now let go of, to move yourself ahead (on to bigger and better things)?

You do not need to tell the person about the steps you are taking—nor does forgiving them condone the behavior. You are simply ridding yourself of excess energy baggage, which can slow you down on your journey ahead.

Person/Situation: _____

Decision/Action I will take:

_____
_____
_____
_____

Person/Situation: _____

Decision/Action I will take:

_____
_____
_____
_____

Person/Situation: _____

Decision/Action I will take:

_____
_____
_____

_____

_____

Although time management, sound strategy, and focused determination are critical to managing a multi-passionate existence, energy is of utmost importance: without it, you will continue to want and dream and wish and talk about your passions, but you may not have the stamina to set up (and live out) the coordinated systems that multi-passionate living involves.

NOTES:

Ideas into Action: Reflective Planning

One of my first jobs in the corporate world involved sales. After weekly pep meetings, we were sternly reminded, "Do not confuse activity with results."

If you have found yourself procrastinating or lacking the motivation to do what you thought you wanted to do, take heart. Review your list of possible energy leaks. If you have already addressed them, and yet still find it hard to get into the passions you thought you'd like to explore, then it's time to rethink the goals that you have set. Are these passions still current to your life right now? Or have you gotten so used to wanting to pursue a specific set of passions that, over time, they have become outdated without you realizing it? People change, sometimes over a short period of time, or in subtle ways. It could be that an idea you were first enthused about—even fairly recently—is no longer hitting the mark, which is reflecting in a mysterious lack of drive to put it into action.

Exercise:

Find a quiet spot, and unplug yourself from any distractions (phone, computer, TV). Remind yourself that everything is ok, and that it is normal to go back and re-assess goals on a frequent basis. The more you re-assess, the more you narrow down and get closer to the sweet spot of finding your true passion blend for right now.

Next, envision your life as a clean slate. You are not bogged down by any endeavors you have already begun or invested into. Picture yourself starting from scratch, in a good way. A blank canvas for you to design.

Now, ask yourself these questions, spending time on each one individually, until you have arrived at an emerging vision.

What would I be doing right now, if I could get started immediately?

What would I choose to do if failure was not possible?

What would my days look like if resources were not an issue?

What would I be emboldened to do if I had complete support from my friends and family—or if none of that even mattered while I did my thing?

As your new vision emerges, write it down in the space provided, or in your *Rainbow Blueprint Action Journal*, if you are using it. This fresh vision is the best snapshot of who you are at this very moment. You need not feel obligated or stay bogged down with outdated versions of yourself simply based on a web of endeavors you have already built up. There are ways to unload these things, if necessary. You can sell items and step back from projects that no longer reflect who you are, or even just tweak a few things in your existing repertoire of activities to reflect your current, most authentic self. This is an effective way to shed layers that you may have been holding onto, but are no longer serving you.

NOTES:

Your Personal Passion Blend

Below is a series of exercises that will lead you to what I call your Personal Passion Blend. The first two steps are helpful if you have not yet defined your primary passions. You already know you have many interests but you will make more headway with each passion by gaining clarity by prioritizing your passions. Which of your passions are of primary interest? Which are more of the "supporting cast," passions you sometimes enjoy if the opportunity arises to look into them?

After completing the first two steps of the exercise, you will be able to integrate your passions and piece together groupings of ideal endeavors, your Personal Passion Blend.

STEP ONE: Choose five favorite activities

What are your five favorite activities – regardless of topic area? For example, researching, traveling, and organizing are all activities, but they are not tied to a specific industry or a single topic area.

Circle five of your favorite activities below. If you would like to select additional ones, underline those. You can also add activities not listed by using the blanks provided at the end of the suggestion list.

Public speaking	Physical activity	Decorating	Manual projects
One-on-one communications (i.e., consulting, coaching, counseling)	Care giving	Teaching/Training	Gardening/Nature-based activities
Writing	Reading	Dancing	Traveling
Researching	Reporting/ Compiling	Singing/Theatre/ Musical performance	Fundraising/Recruiting
Organizing	Cooking/Baking	Praying/Meditating	Selling/Marketing
Leading/Mentoring/ Directing/Managing (of people)	Fine Dining and Spirits	Visiting monuments or museums	Planning

| Logistics/Managing (of tasks) | Socializing/ Entertaining | Collecting | Documenting/ Journalistic |

My preferred activities were not listed. I am passionate about these activities:

_____ _____ _____

_____ _____ _____

_____ _____ _____

Overall, my five favorite activities are:

_____ _____ _____

_____ _____

My additional favorites are:

_____ _____ _____

STEP TWO: Choose five favorite topics or industries

Now it is time to choose five areas of interest. Think of specific topics or industries that interest you most, regardless of what you would be doing within those areas. For example, opera, U.S. history and leadership skills are all topics of interest. At this stage, do not assign the role performed for each. Just think about your favorite topics, not what you would be doing within those fields.

Circle five of your favorite topics below, and add the necessary details. For instance, if you love American History or Civil War History, then under the "History" heading, you would complete the blank line with "American" or "Civil War." The idea is to get specific about your favorite topic areas (without yet committing to what you would do with those passions).

If you would like to select additional topics beyond your five favorites, underline those. With the virtually limitless nature of topics and sub-topics, you can also add activities not listed by using the group of blanks below the chart.

Circle five and complete the blank with specific details about your chosen topics.

History Specifically, _____	**Leadership & Management** Specifically, _____
Foreign Languages Specifically, _____	**Teamwork** Specifically, _____
Gardening & Botany Specifically, _____	**Legal/Investigative** Specifically, _____
Biological & Medical Specifically, _____	**Science** Specifically, _____
Music Specifically, _____	**Automotive & Machines** Specifically, _____
Animals Specifically, _____	**Psychology** Specifically, _____
Children Specifically, _____	**Books & Literary** Specifically, _____
Elderly & Geriatric Specifically, _____	**Computers & Technology** Specifically, _____
Psychology Specifically, _____	**Crafts** Specifically, _____
Art Specifically, _____	**Genealogy/Family History** Specifically, _____

Nature & Wilderness Specifically, _____ **Food/Culinary** Specifically, _____ **Wine & Spirits** Specifically, _____ **Sports** Specifically, _____ **Culture & Diversity** Specifically, _____ **Entrepreneurship** Specifically, _____	**Movies** Specifically, _____ **Graphic Arts & Design** Specifically, _____ **Fashion & Image** Specifically, _____ **Country/Location** (destination-specific) Specifically, _____ **Wedding & Special Events** Specifically, _____ **Internet Marketing & Information Products** Specifically, _____

Favorite topics not listed:

_____

Specifically, _____

_____

Specifically, _____

_____

Specifically, _____

_____

Specifically, _____

_____

Specifically, _____

Overall, my five favorite topic areas are:

_____   _____   _____

_____   _____

My additional favorites are:

_____   _____   _____

STEP THREE: Forming your Personal Passion Blend

This step involves piecing together your ideal activities with the topics or industries you are most passionate about. Just as automotive enthusiasts enjoy putting together their ideal car piece by piece, in a careful and customized way, think of the information from the preceding two steps as your inventory of highly prized components. In what ways can you combine your favorite areas from Step One and Step Two? The result is your Personal Passion Blend.

It is natural that this step may take you some time. Do not rush it; it may take several sittings, or may even take months of reflection and trial-and-error (on paper or in practice). Remember that your ideal combinations may not necessarily involve all components at once, either from the activity or topic category; nor is there a "right" way (or number of activities) to incorporate within each topic area.

One approach is to set up a paper (or a spreadsheet) with each topic area laid out across the top. In a "reserve" area, you can list the possible activities. Then, one by one, consider each topic and the possible activities that would complement that endeavor. Be creative – you can forge your own career and invent opportunities that were not there before!

The Master Venture List

Sometimes, writing down what has been whizzing around in your head is the first step towards quieting the mind. The nice part about writing these ideas down is that they are not lost; they have not been forgotten. They are simply being transferred to a tangible form, which you can review at any time. Writing down, reviewing, and even updating your list can help you to clarify your thoughts and organize your efforts.

Also, just like the advice about packing away clothing that is out-of-season to make more room in our closets for new items, placing non-immediate projects on your Master Venture List allows you to "make room" in your mind for only the most current projects and ideas. Like a computer, you can function best when you are not weighed down with a lot of background programs that can slow you down or distract you.

Let's get started.

Write down, in flowing, brainstorming fashion, all of the projects, traveling, hobbies, careers, relationships, and other goals you would like to accomplish in life. You can mix professional and personal goals. You can even include many of the endeavors from your Personal Passion Blend in the previous exercise. Do not censor or edit anything that comes to mind – just write it down. You can always review your list later and make adjustments.

Choose whichever format works best for you, such as a list format, an outline format, or a mind mapping (visual diagram) format. Although the computer works well for any of these formats, for some people there is no substitute for the natural ease and visceral creativity of a paper and pen. Good, old-fashioned pen and paper are convenient for creating spontaneous diagrams and symbols, or for doing this exercise while "unplugged" and flopped on a comfy couch.

I recommend that you do not yet assign specific dates or years to each. The purpose of this exercise is simply to transfer your ideas from your head to a document, to be kept in a safe and accessible place for periodic review.

Master Venture List Examples

The following are examples of what specific individuals' Master Venture Lists may look like, shown in list format, outline format, and mind mapping format.

LIST FORMAT

A list format (non-categorized) might look like this:

Learn Italian

Travel to Italy and France

Earn my CPA

Read Stieg Larsson's trilogy

Learn to play golf

Own my own horse

Become Senior Partner

Write a mystery novel involving horses

Take Salsa dance lessons

Become SCUBA certified

Start a non-profit to help orphans

Visit the Taj Mahal

Adopt two Greyhounds from animal shelter

OUTLINE FORMAT

If you prefer a tier-based approach, you can use an outline format like this:

I. Career

    a. Obtain an MBA in International Business

    b. Research global corporations

    c. Transition into international business development

        i. China

        ii. India

II. Photography

    a. Own a (dream camera type here)

    b. Take African safari

        i. Wildlife photos

        ii. Serengeti landscape photos

    c. Photography website

        i. Sell prints

        ii. Note cards

    d. Photography exhibit

        i. (Name of Gallery/Venue 1)

        ii. (Name of Gallery/Venue 2)

        iii. (Name of Gallery/Venue 3)

    e. Get featured in major publications

        i. National Geographic

        ii. Outside magazine

        iii. Audubon magazine

III. Family

    a. College for Emily

    b. Coach soccer for Matthew's team

    c. 20th anniversary trip

IV. Books to write

    a. Novel – historical fiction (Northwest territories)

    b. Memoirs (include safari adventure and 2006 trip to Brazil)

MIND MAPPING FORMAT

Mind mapping is a visual method of relating and organizing topics and subtopics around a central theme, or from one starting point. A mind mapping format might look like this:

Mind map below courtesy of XMind (xmind.net)

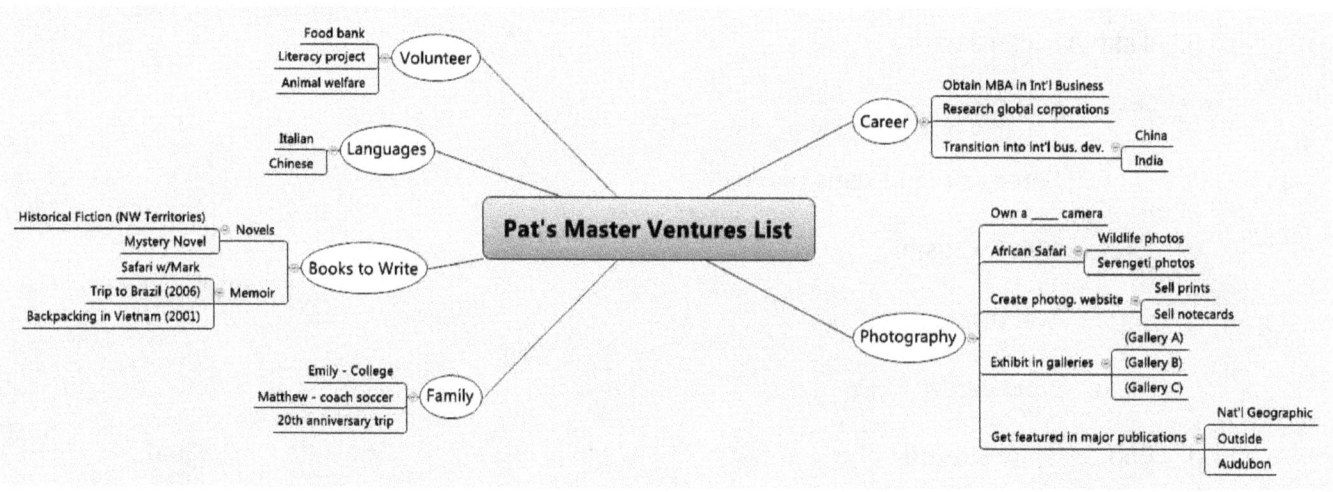

Finally, step back and review your Master Venture List. Are there any areas that seem to stand out? For instance, are some areas much more detailed than others, or with many steps and options? In the example of Pat's Master Venture List, above, we see that photography and writing books seem to have the most components. However, only Pat can decide if the detail factor is enough to make these the top priorities. Pat may decide that family, career, and/or languages are of utmost priority. This is a personal decision, and very much an art, as much as a science.

Keep these factors in mind—length, detail, and personal priority level of each passion—as indicators of your core passions to focus upon as we move into the next exercise: *The Passion Priority Matrix & Weekly Assessments.*

> ### A Note About Mind Mapping:
>
> Pen and paper are classics, but if you prefer an editable, digital canvas for your visual brainstorming, there are a number of mind mapping software providers available online, some of them free.
>
> Each type of software has slightly different features and looks (such as color-coding, icons, shapes, and map formats) so you might want to try them and compare. I personally use XMind (xmind.net), as it is easy to use, has numerous features (including multi-format image export), and has a free and inexpensive Pro option. Here are the websites of several popular brands:
>
> | | |
> |---|---|
> | **XMind.net** | **iMindMap.com** |
> | **MindJet.com** | **Bubbl.us** |
> | **MindMeister.com** | **Mindomo.com** |
> | **SmartDraw.com** | **EDrawSoft.com** |

The Passion Priority Matrix

& Weekly Assessments

The exercises until this point involved intense sessions of strategy and self-analysis. They have built up to a knowledge of yourself and the key pool of passions we will call your Core Passions. But to promote lasting change there needs to be an ongoing effort to manage (and enjoy) your passions in a manner that is both fulfilling and productive. Welcome to *The Passion Priority Matrix* and its complementary counterpart, the *Weekly Assessments*.

I have been using the *Passion Priority Matrix* for years (even before I called it anything), and growing up, it has truly been a life-saver for me when no other tool could manage all that was whirling in my mind and heart at once. And now, my clients love it.

While every exercise in this workbook is important, *The Passion Priority Matrix* is arguably the heart of the workbook. Why? Just the act of assessing, maintaining, executing, and revising your multi-passion management plan, week in and week out, produces a clarity and confidence that allows the Multi-Passionate Professional to remain on task and happy. Coupled with the *Weekly Assessment,* this technique keeps the MPP fresh and current, as the questions probe weekly into your commitment level for each passion.

The Passion Priority Matrix technique is simple. Pick four of your most urgent or passionate categories for the coming week (this is the key to remember: it is just for one week at a time. I know—you have SO many more than four passions; but think in terms of week-long compartments. You can always change out some or all of the passions the following week, depending on how you feel and on the nature of your passion goals.

Why four Core Passions?

If you can manage more than four over the course of a week, that is fantastic. Add more columns and go for it. But the four Core Passions were designed based on my own experience over many years. It seems that this is not only my personal "magic number," but also that of many of my coaching clients.

With more than four Core Passions assigned in a given week, the Passion Sub-Task lists cannot become deeply engaged for most working folks; the result is only a superficial touch upon each passion. Again, if you do not mind that, then find your own "magic number."

What about less than four Core Passions in a week?

With less than four Core Passions assigned in a week, there needs to be depth and active involvement in each passion, or MPPs can feel bored or antsy. But if you design a rich and challenging list of Passion Sub-Tasks for these lone Core Passions, the results can be remarkable. The advantage to focusing on only two or three Core Passions in a week is that there can be significant headway made in the goals of these areas—and for those who have been feeling torn or scattered for a while, this can be a nice change.

So here are the steps to *The Passion Priority Matrix:*

1. Decide on your Core Passions for the week (up to four on the chart).
2. Write out your Core Passions along the top (horizontal) axis of *The Passion Priority Matrix*.
3. Next, write down vertically, under each Core Passion, all that you would feasibly like to accomplish for each Core Passion in the coming week. Think of it as your passion "to do list" for the week, organized by category (above it). I have included up to eight Passion Sub-Tasks for each of the Core Passions.

Some Multi-Passionate Professionals like to sit down on a Sunday and complete the *Weekly Assessment* as they reflect on the week before. Create diagram of this (blank), followed by planning their *Passion Priority Matrix* for the new week ahead. It doesn't matter which day you choose, but I recommend sticking to the same day each week for consistency and structure.

BONUS: *The Passion Priority Matrix* can be used to break down large projects, using each Core Passion column as a sub-category of one larger job. This matrix is also an effective business planning technique to break through a cyclical "chicken and egg" feeling, when there are multiple "top priorities" and it's hard to know where to begin.

Two Approaches

Your *Passion Priority Matrix* may look different from week to week, and not just because of ever-changing passions on the chart. You may find that one week, your aim is to incorporate as many Core Passions as you can into that week. **Example 1** illustrates how this might look (see diagram). The advantage to this approach is that it allows the MPP the chance to feel that they have engaged in a number of their passions over that week. However, the trade-off is that—unless you have an abundance of time—the number of Passion Sub-Tasks that can be accomplished for each of the Core Passions is limited.

Conversely, **Example 2** shows what can be done when only a couple of Core Passions are assigned for the week. In our example, the MPP has chosen to focus on her food blog and on training for a marathon (a beneficial combination, in any case!). This matrix is heavy on the Passion Sub-Tasks; the MPP will make significant headway with her blogging tasks (posting, editing photos, interviewing a chef, etc.) and with her marathon training, research, purchasing gel shoes, etc. However, with the in-depth approach for these two Core Passions, she will not have much time to officially pursue the other Core Passions for that week.

You may find that you gravitate towards one approach more than the other; or the balance of Core Passions and Passion Sub-Tasks may continue to fluctuate from week to week. But guess what? The good news is that no matter what, you only have to decide in one-week increments. Most passions will still be there in seven days—and just think of what you can accomplish with a focused, organized plan, and the liberating feeling that you do *not* need to haul around *all* of your passions at once! Just pick a few for this week, and then revisit your priorities, with the help of your *Weekly Assessment,* in preparation for the following week.

Example 1

Week of 3/28

Core Passions

	A Animal Shelter	B Painting	C Cert.	D Arts Events
Passion Sub-Tasks 1	Mon/Wed - Volunteer @shelter	Measure living rm wall above fireplace	Buy certification Textbook & wkbk	Faculty chamber concert @ ASU
2	Send e-blast re: Spring fundraiser	pick canvas size & buy (gallery wrap)	Thurs. 6-9 pm Prep course	See "Our Town" Sat. night w/Zue
3		Finish sketching pomegranate series		

Example 2

The next example illustrates the use of the Passion Priority Matrix with just two Core Passions for the week, but with a heavy emphasis on each of them. Here, the MPP chose to focus on blogging and marathon training for the week, but has assigned each to a robust list of Passion Sub-Tasks. As you turn the page beyond, you will find your own *Passion Priority Matrix and Weekly Assessments* all set up and ready to go.

Week of 5/14

Core Passions

	A Blog	B Marathon Prep	C	D
1	Brainstorm topics	Email Beth re: training sched.		
2	Categorize new topics	Get new shoes - gel soles		
3	Sort through menus from trip	Research mileage pattern training		
4	Unload/Upload pics from camera	Try long run on Saturday		
5	Edit pics/PShop	Register for SJ		
6	Interview Chef Pierre for eclair review			
7	Write/post for Mon/Wed/Fri			
8	Restaurant Week Sponsorship			

Passion Sub-Tasks

Week of _____

Core Passions

	A	B	C	D
1				
2				
3				
4				
5				
6				
7				
8				

Passion Sub-Tasks

Weekly Assessment

Top focus for this week: _____

Ongoing projects/Carry-over projects:
_____
_____
_____
_____

Projects to be completed within this week:
_____
_____
_____
_____

Weekly Summary:
_____
_____
_____
_____

What went well:
_____
_____
_____
_____

Areas to improve upon:
_____
_____
_____
_____

Core Passion Assessment:

Are there any passion priorities that can be downgraded at this time?
_____
_____
_____

Are there any passion priorities that have increased in the last week?
_____
_____
_____

Week of _____

Core Passions

	A	B	C	D
1				
2				
3				
4				
5				
6				
7				
8				

Passion Sub-Tasks

Weekly Assessment

Top focus for this week: _____

Ongoing projects/Carry-over projects:
_____
_____
_____
_____

Projects to be completed within this week:
_____
_____
_____
_____

Weekly Summary:
_____
_____
_____
_____

What went well:
_____
_____
_____
_____

Areas to improve upon:
_____
_____
_____
_____

Core Passion Assessment:

Are there any passion priorities that can be downgraded at this time?
_____
_____
_____
_____

Are there any passion priorities that have increased in the last week?
_____
_____
_____
_____

Week of _____

Core Passions

	A	B	C	D
1				
2				
3				
4				
5				
6				
7				
8				

Passion Sub-Tasks

Weekly Assessment

Top focus for this week: _____

Ongoing projects/Carry-over projects:
_____
_____
_____
_____

Projects to be completed within this week:
_____
_____
_____
_____

Weekly Summary:
_____
_____
_____
_____

What went well:
_____
_____
_____
_____

Areas to improve upon:
_____
_____
_____
_____

Core Passion Assessment:

Are there any passion priorities that can be downgraded at this time?
_____
_____
_____

Are there any passion priorities that have increased in the last week?
_____
_____
_____

Week of _____

Core Passions

	A	B	C	D
1				
2				
3				
4				
5				
6				
7				
8				

Passion Sub-Tasks

Weekly Assessment

Top focus for this week: _____

Ongoing projects/Carry-over projects:
_____
_____
_____
_____

Projects to be completed within this week:
_____
_____
_____
_____

Weekly Summary:
_____
_____
_____
_____

What went well:
_____
_____
_____
_____

Areas to improve upon:
_____
_____
_____
_____

Core Passion Assessment:

Are there any passion priorities that can be downgraded at this time?
_____
_____
_____

Are there any passion priorities that have increased in the last week?
_____
_____
_____

Week of _____

Core Passions

	A	B	C	D
1				
2				
3				
4				
5				
6				
7				
8				

Passion Sub-Tasks

Weekly Assessment

Top focus for this week: _____

Ongoing projects/Carry-over projects:
_____
_____
_____
_____

Projects to be completed within this week:
_____
_____
_____
_____

Weekly Summary:
_____
_____
_____
_____

What went well:
_____
_____
_____
_____

Areas to improve upon:
_____
_____
_____
_____

Core Passion Assessment:

Are there any passion priorities that can be downgraded at this time?
_____
_____
_____

Are there any passion priorities that have increased in the last week?
_____
_____
_____

Week of _____

Core Passions

	A	B	C	D
1				
2				
3				
4				
5				
6				
7				
8				

Passion Sub-Tasks

Weekly Assessment

Top focus for this week: _____

Ongoing projects/Carry-over projects:
_____
_____
_____
_____

Projects to be completed within this week:
_____
_____
_____
_____

Weekly Summary:
_____
_____
_____
_____

What went well:
_____
_____
_____
_____

Areas to improve upon:
_____
_____
_____
_____

Core Passion Assessment:

Are there any passion priorities that can be downgraded at this time?
_____
_____
_____

Are there any passion priorities that have increased in the last week?
_____
_____
_____

Week of _____

Core Passions

	A	B	C	D
1				
2				
3				
4				
5				
6				
7				
8				

Passion Sub-Tasks

Weekly Assessment

Top focus for this week: _____

Ongoing projects/Carry-over projects:
_____
_____
_____
_____

Projects to be completed within this week:
_____
_____
_____
_____

Weekly Summary:
_____
_____
_____
_____

What went well:
_____
_____
_____
_____

Areas to improve upon:
_____
_____
_____
_____

Core Passion Assessment:

Are there any passion priorities that can be downgraded at this time?
_____
_____
_____
_____

Are there any passion priorities that have increased in the last week?
_____
_____
_____
_____

Week of _____

Core Passions

	A	B	C	D
1				
2				
3				
4				
5				
6				
7				
8				

Passion Sub-Tasks

Weekly Assessment

Top focus for this week: _____

Ongoing projects/Carry-over projects:
_____
_____
_____
_____

Projects to be completed within this week:
_____
_____
_____
_____

Weekly Summary:
_____
_____
_____
_____

What went well:
_____
_____
_____
_____

Areas to improve upon:
_____
_____
_____
_____

Core Passion Assessment:

Are there any passion priorities that can be downgraded at this time?
_____
_____
_____
_____

Are there any passion priorities that have increased in the last week?
_____
_____
_____
_____

Week of _____

Core Passions

	A	B	C	D
1				
2				
3				
4				
5				
6				
7				
8				

Passion Sub-Tasks

Weekly Assessment

Top focus for this week: _____

Ongoing projects/Carry-over projects:
_____
_____
_____
_____

Projects to be completed within this week:
_____
_____
_____
_____

Weekly Summary:
_____
_____
_____
_____

What went well:
_____
_____
_____
_____

Areas to improve upon:
_____
_____
_____
_____

Core Passion Assessment:

Are there any passion priorities that can be downgraded at this time?
_____
_____
_____
_____

Are there any passion priorities that have increased in the last week?
_____
_____
_____
_____

Week of _____

Core Passions

	A	B	C	D
1				
2				
3				
4				
5				
6				
7				
8				

Passion Sub-Tasks

Weekly Assessment

Top focus for this week: _____

Ongoing projects/Carry-over projects:
_____
_____
_____
_____

Projects to be completed within this week:
_____
_____
_____
_____

Weekly Summary:
_____
_____
_____
_____

What went well:
_____
_____
_____
_____

Areas to improve upon:
_____
_____
_____
_____

Core Passion Assessment:

Are there any passion priorities that can be downgraded at this time?
_____
_____
_____
_____

Are there any passion priorities that have increased in the last week?
_____
_____
_____
_____

Week of _____

Core Passions

	A	B	C	D
1				
2				
3				
4				
5				
6				
7				
8				

Passion Sub-Tasks

Weekly Assessment

Top focus for this week: _____

Ongoing projects/Carry-over projects:
_____
_____
_____
_____

Projects to be completed within this week:
_____
_____
_____
_____

Weekly Summary:
_____
_____
_____
_____

What went well:
_____
_____
_____
_____

Areas to improve upon:
_____
_____
_____
_____

Core Passion Assessment:

Are there any passion priorities that can be downgraded at this time?
_____
_____
_____
_____

Are there any passion priorities that have increased in the last week?
_____
_____
_____
_____

Week of _____

Core Passions

	A	B	C	D
1				
2				
3				
4				
5				
6				
7				
8				

Passion Sub-Tasks

Weekly Assessment

Top focus for this week: _____

Ongoing projects/Carry-over projects:
_____
_____
_____
_____

Projects to be completed within this week:
_____
_____
_____
_____

Weekly Summary:
_____
_____
_____
_____

What went well:
_____
_____
_____
_____

Areas to improve upon:
_____
_____
_____
_____

Core Passion Assessment:

Are there any passion priorities that can be downgraded at this time?
_____
_____
_____
_____

Are there any passion priorities that have increased in the last week?
_____
_____
_____
_____

Week of _____

Core Passions

	A	B	C	D
1				
2				
3				
4				
5				
6				
7				
8				

Passion Sub-Tasks

Weekly Assessment

Top focus for this week: _____

Ongoing projects/Carry-over projects:
_____
_____
_____
_____

Projects to be completed within this week:
_____
_____
_____
_____

Weekly Summary:
_____
_____
_____
_____

What went well:
_____
_____
_____
_____

Areas to improve upon:
_____
_____
_____
_____

Core Passion Assessment:

Are there any passion priorities that can be downgraded at this time?
_____
_____
_____

Are there any passion priorities that have increased in the last week?
_____
_____
_____
_____

Week of _____

Core Passions

	A	B	C	D
1				
2				
3				
4				
5				
6				
7				
8				

Passion Sub-Tasks

Weekly Assessment

Top focus for this week: _____

Ongoing projects/Carry-over projects:
_____
_____
_____
_____

Projects to be completed within this week:
_____
_____
_____
_____

Weekly Summary:
_____
_____
_____
_____

What went well:
_____
_____
_____
_____

Areas to improve upon:
_____
_____
_____
_____

Core Passion Assessment:

Are there any passion priorities that can be downgraded at this time?
_____
_____
_____
_____

Are there any passion priorities that have increased in the last week?
_____
_____
_____
_____

Week of _____

Core Passions

	A	B	C	D
1				
2				
3				
4				
5				
6				
7				
8				

Passion Sub-Tasks

Weekly Assessment

Top focus for this week: _____

Ongoing projects/Carry-over projects:
_____
_____
_____
_____

Projects to be completed within this week:
_____
_____
_____
_____

Weekly Summary:
_____
_____
_____
_____

What went well:
_____
_____
_____
_____

Areas to improve upon:
_____
_____
_____
_____

Core Passion Assessment:

Are there any passion priorities that can be downgraded at this time?
_____
_____
_____
_____

Are there any passion priorities that have increased in the last week?
_____
_____
_____
_____

Week of _____

Core Passions

	A	B	C	D
1				
2				
3				
4				
5				
6				
7				
8				

Passion Sub-Tasks

Weekly Assessment

Top focus for this week: _____

Ongoing projects/Carry-over projects:
_____
_____
_____
_____

Projects to be completed within this week:
_____
_____
_____
_____

Weekly Summary:
_____
_____
_____
_____

What went well:
_____
_____
_____
_____

Areas to improve upon:
_____
_____
_____
_____

Core Passion Assessment:

Are there any passion priorities that can be downgraded at this time?
_____
_____
_____
_____

Are there any passion priorities that have increased in the last week?
_____
_____
_____
_____

Week of _____

Core Passions

	A	B	C	D
1				
2				
3				
4				
5				
6				
7				
8				

Passion Sub-Tasks

Weekly Assessment

Top focus for this week: _____

Ongoing projects/Carry-over projects:
_____
_____
_____
_____

Projects to be completed within this week:
_____
_____
_____
_____

Weekly Summary:
_____
_____
_____
_____

What went well:
_____
_____
_____
_____

Areas to improve upon:
_____
_____
_____
_____

Core Passion Assessment:

Are there any passion priorities that can be downgraded at this time?
_____
_____
_____
_____

Are there any passion priorities that have increased in the last week?
_____
_____
_____
_____

Week of _____

Core Passions

	A	B	C	D
1				
2				
3				
4				
5				
6				
7				
8				

Passion Sub-Tasks

Weekly Assessment

Top focus for this week: _____

Ongoing projects/Carry-over projects:
_____
_____
_____
_____

Projects to be completed within this week:
_____
_____
_____
_____

Weekly Summary:
_____
_____
_____
_____

What went well:
_____
_____
_____
_____

Areas to improve upon:
_____
_____
_____
_____

Core Passion Assessment:

Are there any passion priorities that can be downgraded at this time?
_____
_____
_____
_____

Are there any passion priorities that have increased in the last week?
_____
_____
_____
_____

Week of _____

Core Passions

	A	B	C	D
1				
2				
3				
4				
5				
6				
7				
8				

Passion Sub-Tasks

Weekly Assessment

Top focus for this week: _____

Ongoing projects/Carry-over projects:
_____
_____
_____
_____

Projects to be completed within this week:
_____
_____
_____
_____

Weekly Summary:
_____
_____
_____
_____

What went well:
_____
_____
_____
_____

Areas to improve upon:
_____
_____
_____
_____

Core Passion Assessment:

Are there any passion priorities that can be downgraded at this time?
_____
_____
_____

Are there any passion priorities that have increased in the last week?
_____
_____
_____

Week of _____

Core Passions

	A	B	C	D
1				
2				
3				
4				
5				
6				
7				
8				

Passion Sub-Tasks

Weekly Assessment

Top focus for this week: _____

Ongoing projects/Carry-over projects:
_____
_____
_____
_____

Projects to be completed within this week:
_____
_____
_____
_____

Weekly Summary:
_____
_____
_____
_____

What went well:
_____
_____
_____
_____

Areas to improve upon:
_____
_____
_____
_____

Core Passion Assessment:

Are there any passion priorities that can be downgraded at this time?
_____
_____
_____
_____

Are there any passion priorities that have increased in the last week?
_____
_____
_____
_____

Week of _____

Core Passions

	A	B	C	D
1				
2				
3				
4				
5				
6				
7				
8				

Passion Sub-Tasks

Weekly Assessment

Top focus for this week: _____

Ongoing projects/Carry-over projects:
_____
_____
_____
_____

Projects to be completed within this week:
_____
_____
_____
_____

Weekly Summary:
_____
_____
_____
_____

What went well:
_____
_____
_____
_____

Areas to improve upon:
_____
_____
_____
_____

Core Passion Assessment:

Are there any passion priorities that can be downgraded at this time?
_____
_____
_____
_____

Are there any passion priorities that have increased in the last week?
_____
_____
_____
_____

Week of _____

Core Passions

	A	B	C	D
1				
2				
3				
4				
5				
6				
7				
8				

Passion Sub-Tasks

Weekly Assessment

Top focus for this week: _____

Ongoing projects/Carry-over projects:
_____
_____
_____
_____

Projects to be completed within this week:
_____
_____
_____
_____

Weekly Summary:
_____
_____
_____
_____

What went well:
_____
_____
_____
_____

Areas to improve upon:
_____
_____
_____
_____

Core Passion Assessment:

Are there any passion priorities that can be downgraded at this time?
_____
_____
_____
_____

Are there any passion priorities that have increased in the last week?
_____
_____
_____
_____

Week of _____

Core Passions

	A	B	C	D
1				
2				
3				
4				
5				
6				
7				
8				

Passion Sub-Tasks

Weekly Assessment

Top focus for this week: _____

Ongoing projects/Carry-over projects:
_____
_____
_____
_____

Projects to be completed within this week:
_____
_____
_____
_____

Weekly Summary:
_____
_____
_____
_____

What went well:
_____
_____
_____
_____

Areas to improve upon:
_____
_____
_____
_____

Core Passion Assessment:

Are there any passion priorities that can be downgraded at this time?
_____
_____
_____
_____

Are there any passion priorities that have increased in the last week?
_____
_____
_____
_____

Week of _____

Core Passions

	A	B	C	D
1				
2				
3				
4				
5				
6				
7				
8				

Passion Sub-Tasks

Weekly Assessment

Top focus for this week: _____

Ongoing projects/Carry-over projects:
_____
_____
_____
_____

Projects to be completed within this week:
_____
_____
_____
_____

Weekly Summary:
_____
_____
_____
_____

What went well:
_____
_____
_____
_____

Areas to improve upon:
_____
_____
_____
_____

Core Passion Assessment:

Are there any passion priorities that can be downgraded at this time?
_____
_____
_____
_____

Are there any passion priorities that have increased in the last week?
_____
_____
_____
_____

Week of _____

Core Passions

	A	B	C	D
1				
2				
3				
4				
5				
6				
7				
8				

Passion Sub-Tasks

Weekly Assessment

Top focus for this week: _____

Ongoing projects/Carry-over projects:
_____
_____
_____
_____

Projects to be completed within this week:
_____
_____
_____
_____

Weekly Summary:
_____
_____
_____
_____

What went well:
_____
_____
_____
_____

Areas to improve upon:
_____
_____
_____
_____

Core Passion Assessment:

Are there any passion priorities that can be downgraded at this time?
_____
_____
_____
_____

Are there any passion priorities that have increased in the last week?
_____
_____
_____
_____

Week of _____

Core Passions

	A	B	C	D
1				
2				
3				
4				
5				
6				
7				
8				

Passion Sub-Tasks

Weekly Assessment

Top focus for this week: _____

Ongoing projects/Carry-over projects:
_____
_____
_____
_____

Projects to be completed within this week:
_____
_____
_____
_____

Weekly Summary:
_____
_____
_____
_____

What went well:
_____
_____
_____
_____

Areas to improve upon:
_____
_____
_____
_____

Core Passion Assessment:

Are there any passion priorities that can be downgraded at this time?
_____
_____
_____

Are there any passion priorities that have increased in the last week?
_____
_____
_____

Week of _____

Core Passions

	A	B	C	D
1				
2				
3				
4				
5				
6				
7				
8				

Passion Sub-Tasks

Weekly Assessment

Top focus for this week: _____

Ongoing projects/Carry-over projects:
_____
_____
_____
_____

Projects to be completed within this week:
_____
_____
_____
_____

Weekly Summary:
_____
_____
_____
_____

What went well:
_____
_____
_____
_____

Areas to improve upon:
_____
_____
_____
_____

Core Passion Assessment:

Are there any passion priorities that can be downgraded at this time?
_____
_____
_____
_____

Are there any passion priorities that have increased in the last week?
_____
_____
_____
_____

Week of _____

Core Passions

	A	B	C	D
1				
2				
3				
4				
5				
6				
7				
8				

Passion Sub-Tasks

Weekly Assessment

Top focus for this week: _____

Ongoing projects/Carry-over projects:
_____
_____
_____
_____

Projects to be completed within this week:
_____
_____
_____
_____

Weekly Summary:
_____
_____
_____
_____

What went well:
_____
_____
_____
_____

Areas to improve upon:
_____
_____
_____
_____

Core Passion Assessment:

Are there any passion priorities that can be downgraded at this time?
_____
_____
_____

Are there any passion priorities that have increased in the last week?
_____
_____
_____

Week of _____

Core Passions

	A	B	C	D
1				
2				
3				
4				
5				
6				
7				
8				

Passion Sub-Tasks

Weekly Assessment

Top focus for this week: _____

Ongoing projects/Carry-over projects:
_____
_____
_____
_____

Projects to be completed within this week:
_____
_____
_____
_____

Weekly Summary:
_____
_____
_____
_____

What went well:
_____
_____
_____
_____

Areas to improve upon:
_____
_____
_____
_____

Core Passion Assessment:

Are there any passion priorities that can be downgraded at this time?
_____
_____
_____

Are there any passion priorities that have increased in the last week?
_____
_____
_____

Week of _____

Core Passions

	A	B	C	D
1				
2				
3				
4				
5				
6				
7				
8				

Passion Sub-Tasks

Weekly Assessment

Top focus for this week: _____

Ongoing projects/Carry-over projects:
_____
_____
_____
_____

Projects to be completed within this week:
_____
_____
_____
_____

Weekly Summary:
_____
_____
_____
_____

What went well:
_____
_____
_____
_____

Areas to improve upon:
_____
_____
_____
_____

Core Passion Assessment:

Are there any passion priorities that can be downgraded at this time?
_____
_____
_____
_____

Are there any passion priorities that have increased in the last week?
_____
_____
_____
_____

Week of _____

Core Passions

	A	B	C	D
1				
2				
3				
4				
5				
6				
7				
8				

Passion Sub-Tasks

Weekly Assessment

Top focus for this week: _____

Ongoing projects/Carry-over projects:
_____
_____
_____
_____

Projects to be completed within this week:
_____
_____
_____
_____

Weekly Summary:
_____
_____
_____
_____

What went well:
_____
_____
_____
_____

Areas to improve upon:
_____
_____
_____
_____

Core Passion Assessment:

Are there any passion priorities that can be downgraded at this time?
_____
_____
_____
_____

Are there any passion priorities that have increased in the last week?
_____
_____
_____
_____

Week of _____

Core Passions

	A	B	C	D
1				
2				
3				
4				
5				
6				
7				
8				

Passion Sub-Tasks

Weekly Assessment

Top focus for this week: _____

Ongoing projects/Carry-over projects:
_____
_____
_____
_____

Projects to be completed within this week:
_____
_____
_____
_____

Weekly Summary:
_____
_____
_____
_____

What went well:
_____
_____
_____
_____

Areas to improve upon:
_____
_____
_____
_____

Core Passion Assessment:

Are there any passion priorities that can be downgraded at this time?
_____
_____
_____
_____

Are there any passion priorities that have increased in the last week?
_____
_____
_____
_____

Week of _____

Core Passions

	A	B	C	D
1				
2				
3				
4				
5				
6				
7				
8				

Passion Sub-Tasks

Weekly Assessment

Top focus for this week: _____

Ongoing projects/Carry-over projects:
_____
_____
_____
_____

Projects to be completed within this week:
_____
_____
_____
_____

Weekly Summary:
_____
_____
_____
_____

What went well:
_____
_____
_____
_____

Areas to improve upon:
_____
_____
_____
_____

Core Passion Assessment:

Are there any passion priorities that can be downgraded at this time?
_____
_____
_____
_____

Are there any passion priorities that have increased in the last week?
_____
_____
_____
_____

Week of _____

Core Passions

	A	B	C	D
1				
2				
3				
4				
5				
6				
7				
8				

Passion Sub-Tasks

Weekly Assessment

Top focus for this week: _____

Ongoing projects/Carry-over projects:
_____
_____
_____
_____

Projects to be completed within this week:
_____
_____
_____
_____

Weekly Summary:
_____
_____
_____
_____

What went well:
_____
_____
_____
_____

Areas to improve upon:
_____
_____
_____
_____

Core Passion Assessment:

Are there any passion priorities that can be downgraded at this time?
_____
_____
_____

Are there any passion priorities that have increased in the last week?
_____
_____
_____

Week of _____

Core Passions

	A	B	C	D
1				
2				
3				
4				
5				
6				
7				
8				

Passion Sub-Tasks

Weekly Assessment

Top focus for this week: _____

Ongoing projects/Carry-over projects:
_____
_____
_____
_____

Projects to be completed within this week:
_____
_____
_____
_____

Weekly Summary:
_____
_____
_____
_____

What went well:
_____
_____
_____
_____

Areas to improve upon:
_____
_____
_____
_____

Core Passion Assessment:

Are there any passion priorities that can be downgraded at this time?
_____
_____
_____
_____

Are there any passion priorities that have increased in the last week?
_____
_____
_____
_____

Week of _____

Core Passions

	A	B	C	D
1				
2				
3				
4				
5				
6				
7				
8				

Passion Sub-Tasks

Weekly Assessment

Top focus for this week: _____

Ongoing projects/Carry-over projects:
_____
_____
_____
_____

Projects to be completed within this week:
_____
_____
_____
_____

Weekly Summary:
_____
_____
_____
_____

What went well:
_____
_____
_____
_____

Areas to improve upon:
_____
_____
_____
_____

Core Passion Assessment:

Are there any passion priorities that can be downgraded at this time?
_____
_____
_____
_____

Are there any passion priorities that have increased in the last week?
_____
_____
_____
_____

Week of _____

Core Passions

	A	B	C	D
1				
2				
3				
4				
5				
6				
7				
8				

Passion Sub-Tasks

Weekly Assessment

Top focus for this week: _____

Ongoing projects/Carry-over projects:
_____
_____
_____
_____

Projects to be completed within this week:
_____
_____
_____
_____

Weekly Summary:
_____
_____
_____
_____

What went well:
_____
_____
_____
_____

Areas to improve upon:
_____
_____
_____
_____

Core Passion Assessment:

Are there any passion priorities that can be downgraded at this time?
_____
_____
_____
_____

Are there any passion priorities that have increased in the last week?
_____
_____
_____
_____

Week of _____

Core Passions

	A	B	C	D
1				
2				
3				
4				
5				
6				
7				
8				

Passion Sub-Tasks

Weekly Assessment

Top focus for this week: _____

Ongoing projects/Carry-over projects:
_____
_____
_____
_____

Projects to be completed within this week:
_____
_____
_____
_____

Weekly Summary:
_____
_____
_____
_____

What went well:
_____
_____
_____
_____

Areas to improve upon:
_____
_____
_____
_____

Core Passion Assessment:

Are there any passion priorities that can be downgraded at this time?
_____
_____
_____
_____

Are there any passion priorities that have increased in the last week?
_____
_____
_____
_____

Week of _____

Core Passions

	A	B	C	D
1				
2				
3				
4				
5				
6				
7				
8				

Passion Sub-Tasks

Weekly Assessment

Top focus for this week: _____

Ongoing projects/Carry-over projects:
_____
_____
_____
_____

Projects to be completed within this week:
_____
_____
_____
_____

Weekly Summary:
_____
_____
_____
_____

What went well:
_____
_____
_____
_____

Areas to improve upon:
_____
_____
_____
_____

Core Passion Assessment:

Are there any passion priorities that can be downgraded at this time?
_____
_____
_____

Are there any passion priorities that have increased in the last week?
_____
_____
_____

Week of _____

Core Passions

	A	B	C	D
1				
2				
3				
4				
5				
6				
7				
8				

Passion Sub-Tasks

Weekly Assessment

Top focus for this week: _____

Ongoing projects/Carry-over projects:
_____
_____
_____
_____

Projects to be completed within this week:
_____
_____
_____
_____

Weekly Summary:
_____
_____
_____
_____

What went well:
_____
_____
_____
_____

Areas to improve upon:
_____
_____
_____
_____

Core Passion Assessment:

Are there any passion priorities that can be downgraded at this time?
_____
_____
_____

Are there any passion priorities that have increased in the last week?
_____
_____
_____

Week of _____

Core Passions

	A	B	C	D
1				
2				
3				
4				
5				
6				
7				
8				

Passion Sub-Tasks

Weekly Assessment

Top focus for this week: _____

Ongoing projects/Carry-over projects:
_____
_____
_____
_____

Projects to be completed within this week:
_____
_____
_____
_____

Weekly Summary:
_____
_____
_____
_____

What went well:
_____
_____
_____
_____

Areas to improve upon:
_____
_____
_____
_____

Core Passion Assessment:

Are there any passion priorities that can be downgraded at this time?
_____
_____
_____

Are there any passion priorities that have increased in the last week?
_____
_____
_____
_____

Week of _____

Core Passions

	A	B	C	D
1				
2				
3				
4				
5				
6				
7				
8				

Passion Sub-Tasks

Weekly Assessment

Top focus for this week: _____

Ongoing projects/Carry-over projects:
_____
_____
_____
_____

Projects to be completed within this week:
_____
_____
_____
_____

Weekly Summary:
_____
_____
_____
_____

What went well:
_____
_____
_____
_____

Areas to improve upon:
_____
_____
_____
_____

Core Passion Assessment:

Are there any passion priorities that can be downgraded at this time?
_____
_____
_____

Are there any passion priorities that have increased in the last week?
_____
_____
_____
_____

Week of _____

Core Passions

	A	B	C	D
1				
2				
3				
4				
5				
6				
7				
8				

Passion Sub-Tasks

Weekly Assessment

Top focus for this week: _____

Ongoing projects/Carry-over projects:
_____
_____
_____
_____

Projects to be completed within this week:
_____
_____
_____
_____

Weekly Summary:
_____
_____
_____
_____

What went well:
_____
_____
_____
_____

Areas to improve upon:
_____
_____
_____
_____

Core Passion Assessment:

Are there any passion priorities that can be downgraded at this time?
_____
_____
_____

Are there any passion priorities that have increased in the last week?
_____
_____
_____

Week of _____.

Core Passions

	A	B	C	D
1				
2				
3				
4				
5				
6				
7				
8				

Passion Sub-Tasks

Weekly Assessment

Top focus for this week: _____

Ongoing projects/Carry-over projects:
_____
_____
_____
_____

Projects to be completed within this week:
_____
_____
_____
_____

Weekly Summary:
_____
_____
_____
_____

What went well:
_____
_____
_____
_____

Areas to improve upon:
_____
_____
_____
_____

Core Passion Assessment:

Are there any passion priorities that can be downgraded at this time?
_____
_____
_____
_____

Are there any passion priorities that have increased in the last week?
_____
_____
_____
_____

Week of _____

Core Passions

	A	B	C	D
1				
2				
3				
4				
5				
6				
7				
8				

Passion Sub-Tasks

Weekly Assessment

Top focus for this week: _____

Ongoing projects/Carry-over projects:
_____
_____
_____
_____

Projects to be completed within this week:
_____
_____
_____
_____

Weekly Summary:
_____
_____
_____
_____

What went well:
_____
_____
_____
_____

Areas to improve upon:
_____
_____
_____
_____

Core Passion Assessment:

Are there any passion priorities that can be downgraded at this time?
_____
_____
_____
_____

Are there any passion priorities that have increased in the last week?
_____
_____
_____
_____

Week of _____

Core Passions

	A	B	C	D
1				
2				
3				
4				
5				
6				
7				
8				

Passion Sub-Tasks

Weekly Assessment

Top focus for this week: _____

Ongoing projects/Carry-over projects:
_____
_____
_____
_____

Projects to be completed within this week:
_____
_____
_____
_____

Weekly Summary:
_____
_____
_____
_____

What went well:
_____
_____
_____
_____

Areas to improve upon:
_____
_____
_____
_____

Core Passion Assessment:

Are there any passion priorities that can be downgraded at this time?
_____
_____
_____

Are there any passion priorities that have increased in the last week?
_____
_____
_____

Week of _____

Core Passions

	A	B	C	D
1				
2				
3				
4				
5				
6				
7				
8				

Passion Sub-Tasks

Weekly Assessment

Top focus for this week: _____

Ongoing projects/Carry-over projects:
_____
_____
_____
_____

Projects to be completed within this week:
_____
_____
_____
_____

Weekly Summary:
_____
_____
_____
_____

What went well:
_____
_____
_____
_____

Areas to improve upon:
_____
_____
_____
_____

Core Passion Assessment:

Are there any passion priorities that can be downgraded at this time?
_____
_____
_____

Are there any passion priorities that have increased in the last week?
_____
_____
_____
_____

Week of _____

Core Passions

	A	B	C	D
1				
2				
3				
4				
5				
6				
7				
8				

Passion Sub-Tasks

Weekly Assessment

Top focus for this week: _____

Ongoing projects/Carry-over projects:
_____
_____
_____
_____

Projects to be completed within this week:
_____
_____
_____
_____

Weekly Summary:
_____
_____
_____
_____

What went well:
_____
_____
_____
_____

Areas to improve upon:
_____
_____
_____
_____

Core Passion Assessment:

Are there any passion priorities that can be downgraded at this time?
_____
_____
_____

Are there any passion priorities that have increased in the last week?
_____
_____
_____

Week of _____

Core Passions

	A	B	C	D
1				
2				
3				
4				
5				
6				
7				
8				

Passion Sub-Tasks

Weekly Assessment

Top focus for this week: _____

Ongoing projects/Carry-over projects:
_____
_____
_____
_____

Projects to be completed within this week:
_____
_____
_____
_____

Weekly Summary:
_____
_____
_____
_____

What went well:
_____
_____
_____
_____

Areas to improve upon:
_____
_____
_____
_____

Core Passion Assessment:

Are there any passion priorities that can be downgraded at this time?
_____
_____
_____

Are there any passion priorities that have increased in the last week?
_____
_____
_____
_____

Week of _____

Core Passions

	A	B	C	D
1				
2				
3				
4				
5				
6				
7				
8				

Passion Sub-Tasks

Weekly Assessment

Top focus for this week: _____

Ongoing projects/Carry-over projects:
_____
_____
_____
_____

Projects to be completed within this week:
_____
_____
_____
_____

Weekly Summary:
_____
_____
_____
_____

What went well:
_____
_____
_____
_____

Areas to improve upon:
_____
_____
_____
_____

Core Passion Assessment:

Are there any passion priorities that can be downgraded at this time?
_____
_____
_____

Are there any passion priorities that have increased in the last week?
_____
_____
_____
_____

Week of _____

Core Passions

	A	B	C	D
1				
2				
3				
4				
5				
6				
7				
8				

Passion Sub-Tasks

Weekly Assessment

Top focus for this week: _____

Ongoing projects/Carry-over projects:
_____
_____
_____
_____

Projects to be completed within this week:
_____
_____
_____
_____

Weekly Summary:
_____
_____
_____
_____

What went well:
_____
_____
_____
_____

Areas to improve upon:
_____
_____
_____
_____

Core Passion Assessment:

Are there any passion priorities that can be downgraded at this time?
_____
_____
_____
_____

Are there any passion priorities that have increased in the last week?
_____
_____
_____
_____

Week of ____________________

Core Passions

Passion Sub-Tasks	A	B	C	D
1				
2				
3				
4				
5				
6				
7				
8				

Weekly Assessment

Top focus for this week: _____

Ongoing projects/Carry-over projects:
_____
_____
_____
_____

Projects to be completed within this week:
_____
_____
_____
_____

Weekly Summary:
_____
_____
_____
_____

What went well:
_____
_____
_____
_____

Areas to improve upon:
_____
_____
_____
_____

Core Passion Assessment:

Are there any passion priorities that can be downgraded at this time?
_____
_____
_____

Are there any passion priorities that have increased in the last week?
_____
_____
_____
_____

Week of _____

Core Passions

	A	B	C	D
1				
2				
3				
4				
5				
6				
7				
8				

Passion Sub-Tasks

Weekly Assessment

Top focus for this week: _____

Ongoing projects/Carry-over projects:
_____
_____
_____
_____

Projects to be completed within this week:
_____
_____
_____
_____

Weekly Summary:
_____
_____
_____
_____

What went well:
_____
_____
_____
_____

Areas to improve upon:
_____
_____
_____
_____

Core Passion Assessment:

Are there any passion priorities that can be downgraded at this time?
_____
_____
_____
_____

Are there any passion priorities that have increased in the last week?
_____
_____
_____
_____

Passion Engagement Inventory

As you complete each week's *Passion Priority Matrix and Weekly Assessment,* keep a tally below of the passions that you were able to engage in. Over time, you should see a rewarding array of your passions listed. This is great news! It is a sign that you are successfully incorporating multiple passions into your life.

I have engaged in the following passions since starting this program on _____

_____

_____

_____

_____

_____

_____

_____

_____

_____

_____

_____

_____

_____

_____

_____

_____

Wrap-Up Review

Congratulations!

You have completed *The GUSTO POWER® Workbook: Tactics and Strategies for the Multi-Passionate Professional*™. This is no small feat. As the workbook's name suggests, you have carried out a series of rigorous exercises and introspective processes that were designed to help you overcome the perennial hurdle of managing numerous passions and talents.

Whether you completed the workbook in its entirety or chose to focus on particular chapters; and whether you stretched your passion management over a period of 52 weeks or used this workbook periodically; and whether you completed this work on your own, or through a GUSTO POWER® workshop or your Human Resources department; give yourself a strong pat on the back. You have achieved a milestone in personal growth and professional development. Many people continue to struggle with the delicate balance of multiple interests, but you have been proactive—and now you can reap the rewards through a more fulfilling and productive life and career.

The knowledge and practice that you have gained are yours forever, and will only continue to blossom as you keep your passions and priorities in focus.

Your Turn

What did *you* think of this experience? As the creator of the GUSTO POWER® program and this workbook (and as a fellow Multi-Passionate Professional™ myself), I am eager to hear your feedback, comments, and your own experiences as a Multi-Passionate Professional.

In order to seal this milestone in your learning, take some time out, find a quiet spot, and reflect upon your recent experience with this workbook. Complete the following questions/survey, either privately for yourself; or you may download an electronic document of this page at **GustoPowerBook.com**, complete it, and send it back to me at **info@GustoPower.com** (with "Workbook" in the subject line). We hold periodic drawings and contests and include those who submit completed feedback forms to us.

Wrap-Up Review & Survey Questions

I would characterize my involvement in this workbook as (circle/highlight one):

Consistently/Frequently involved   Periodically involved, on an as-needed basis

Occasionally involved   Rarely involved

On a scale of 1-10 (10 being the highest), I found the exercises to be effective for my needs:

1   2   3   4   5   6   7   8   9   10

Why this score?
_____
_____
_____

I particularly enjoyed:
_____
_____
_____

I would have liked to see more/less of (please specify):
_____
_____
_____

I completed the exercises in the order they appeared   YES   NO

My favorite exercise was _____

because _____

My least favorite exercise was _____

because _____

Looking back from the time I began using this workbook, I see my skills have improved in these ways:

_____
_____
_____
_____

I would like to continue my work in the following ways: (circle/highlight all that apply)

Revisiting/Continuing the workbook exercises

Join/Form a peer-to-peer network of fellow Multi-Passionate Professionals™ (MPPs)

Receive One-on-One Coaching

Participate in Group Coaching

Attend a Seminar

Read more books about the topic

Listen to an audio program

Hear a live speaker about this topic

Other_____

I could use more information about

_____

My preferred format is

_____

The top 3 ways that The GUSTO POWER® Workbook has helped me:

_____
_____
_____

Name _____

Email _____

Phone # _____

Mailing address_____
_____

May we use your comments (with your name) as testimonials in our materials? YES   NO

Additional comments:

_____
_____
_____
_____

(For electronic submission of the above information, please email to info@GustoPower.com)

I appreciate you taking the time to complete this review, and for taking the GUSTO POWER® journey with me. May you continue to enjoy numerous passions, and the savvy skills to engage in them all!

-Gilat Ben-Dor

About the Author

Gilat Ben-Dor, MBA, CSW is an author, speaker, coach, and the founder of GUSTO POWER®, a leadership development program that helps Multi-Passionate Professionals™ successfully manage their many talents. A creative "multipreneur" herself, Gilat has created several successful businesses, including a wine education firm, a publishing company, and an online emporium featuring her art and photography.

Gilat Ben-Dor's corporate background includes the areas of Human Resources, Training and Development, and Higher Education Administration. Gilat is an adjunct faculty member at a nationally recognized university. She holds an MBA in Global Management and a Certificate of Mediation. She is based in Scottsdale, Arizona.

For more information about Gilat Ben-Dor, visit her central web site, **GilatBen-Dor.com**

To learn more about Gilat Ben-Dor's *GUSTO POWER®* success strategy program for Multi-Passionate Professionals™, and to receive a FREE report about "The Top 5 Mistakes Multi-Passionate Professionals Make," visit **GustoPower.com**

For *The GUSTO POWER® Workbook's* official website, visit **GustoPowerBook.com**

Additional Opportunities

Speaking, Coaching,

Consulting and Workshops

with Gilat Ben-Dor

Your experiences working with The GUSTO POWER® Workbook may have been private and intense, but your new discoveries may benefit your organization, including how to manage multiple passions and projects through planning and action. Imagine sharing your insights and newly honed skills for passion and project management with your company and your network by bringing GUSTO POWER® to your workplace!

Dynamic speaker, author, coach and consultant Gilat Ben-Dor is passionate about bringing more creativity, productivity, and peace of mind to Multi-Passionate Professionals™ and their teams.

Gilat Ben-Dor's presentation and consulting formats include keynote speeches, break-out sessions, workshops/seminars, webinars, internal consulting, and her Platinum one-on-one coaching program.

Suggested participants include:

- Leaders & Managers
- Human Resources Professionals
- Career Counselors/Consultants
- Creative Professionals
- Associations
- Entrepreneurs

For more information about booking Gilat Ben-Dor for your organization,

please email info@GustoPower.com

As a complement to the message of *The GUSTO POWER® Workbook: Tactics and Strategies for the Multi-Passionate Professional™*, Gilat Ben-Dor offers a special presentation:

Celebrate Your Spectrum: The Perks of Being a Multi-Passionate Professional™

Using her diverse background in human resources, training and development, teaching, coaching, and creative entrepreneurship, Gilat Ben-Dor offers this content-rich experience as a hands-on workshop or a traditional keynote presentation. The GUSTO POWER® Workbook and Gilat Ben-Dor's presentation promise to awaken the realm of possibilities for both personal and workplace trajectories.

Additional presentation topics by Gilat Ben-Dor include:

GUSTO POWER®: Power Skills for the Multi-Passionate Professional™

Gilat's signature keynote of the Gusto Power® program, this presentation is ideal for both corporate and entrepreneurial groups. Through engaging stories, humor and pertinent case studies, the audience will take away a new understanding of the benefits of exploring our diverse sets of talents. Participants will learn simple, effective "Power Skills" they can apply immediately to increase personal satisfaction, workplace morale, and professional productivity.

Like a Diamond: The Brilliance and Benefits of Multi-Faceted Careers™

Many of us have been conditioned to believe that professionally, we must only do one thing and be one thing. But this shoe does not fit everyone, and holding back can short-change both ourselves and our organizations. This eye-opening presentation will reveal the untapped potential — and how to unleash it — from each individual, and how this immense pool of hidden talents can result in profitable partnerships and synergies.

Creative Nine-to-Five: Branching Out While Punching In™

Although specialists have traditionally been valued, the definition of a valued employee is rapidly changing. With economic shakedowns and a new corporate landscape, today's MVE (Most Valuable Employee) can do more by calling upon all sides of themselves. This keynote combines case studies, personal experiences, and an uplifting message that celebrates the value employees offer their organization by being multi-faceted professionals.

Book and workbook discounts available for high-volume purchases.

For more details, please email the publisher at info@GilatMedia.com

> To obtain a free report, "The Top 5 Mistakes Multi-Passionate Professionals Make," visit www.GustoPower.com

www.ingramcontent.com/pod-product-compliance
Lightning Source LLC
Chambersburg PA
CBHW080512110426
42742CB00017B/3087